Asser's Life of Alfred the Great

A LOCHINVAR GUIDE

Student's Edition

EILEEN CUNNINGHAM

Edited by Amy Alexander Carmichael

LOCHINVAR GUIDES TO CLASSIC WORKS OF NONFICTION

Table of Contents

Historical Background 1

A Note on Ancient and Medieval Biography 3

Part 1: Family and Youth 5

Part 2: Fighting the Vikings 13

Part 3: Building a Kingdom 19

Introduction

We are thrilled that you have chosen *Lochinvar Guides* as your method of navigating the classic works of nonfiction in western civilization.

Methodology and Worldview

The *Guides* are informed by the classical method of education which emphasizes primary sources of history, the use of syllogistic thinking and logical analysis, and the application of the progymnasmata (early exercises in classical composition). Moreover, the *Guides* are written from a Christian worldview and incorporate Scripture throughout. There is, we believe, no basic incompatibility between these two paradigms. As the world entered the Christian Era, what made the classical method of education so highly adaptable to Christian culture was what Roman historian Cato the Elder (d. AD 149) posited as the purpose of education: to train up *"vir bonus, dicendi peritus"* (i.e., a good man speaking well)—the philosophy which Quintilian used as his foundation in his educational treatise *Institutio Oratorio* (c. AD 95). From the time of Socrates, classical education has always driven students to ground themselves in morals and ethics; what could be more compatible with Christian education? In our own time, of course, Cato's nugget inspires the training not only of good men, but also good *women*, who, it is hoped, can both speak and *write* well. A program with such a methodology and such a purpose helps, we believe, to prepare students to follow in the footsteps of the great Christian orator, Paul of Tarsus, who wrote: "We destroy arguments and every lofty opinion raised against the knowledge of God, and take every thought captive to obey Christ" (2 Cor. 10:5).

Each work which is covered by one of the *Guides* is broken into manageable reading assignments and contains the following features:

- **Historical Background**—information that helps students better understand the work they are reading—e.g., the dynasty into which Charlemagne was born, the proprietary government of the British colonies in America, the Anglo-Saxon heptarchy in which King Alfred operated, etc.

- **Terms**—terms of a cultural or historical nature with which the general reader might not be familiar. What was a *chrisom*, for example? Or, what was the right of sanctuary?

- **Words**—vocabulary which might be new to the reader, presented with pronunciation key, part of speech, definition, and, if necessary, an explanation of archaic usage

- **Identifications**—identifications of people, places, and events which may be unfamiliar. Who were the Merovingians, for example? Or, where is St. George's Channel?

- **Illustrations**—portraits or classic works of art that can foster a more personal response than can unillustrated material

- **Questions**—short answer questions as well as "graduated questions," wherein the student answers a series of objective questions (grammar stage, in the classical tradition) which lead to more subjective questions (logic or rhetoric stage)

- **Diction Analysis**—highlights of effective stylistic techniques which elevate the work above others of its type

- **Nonfiction Strategies**—activities designed to improve certain skills useful in the reading of nonfiction: following transitions, analyzing verb tense, perceiving tone, generating images, taking notes, etc.

- **Adapted Literature Circle Approaches**—special activities which lead the student to make connections, think critically, etc. (see full details below)

- **Composition Topics**—writing about ideas generated by the text; sometimes employing elements of the progymnasmata (the early exercises in classical composition) for which approaches and models are provided

Depending on the class or the individual home school student, a teacher or teaching parent can pick and choose from among the various options—or even substitute alternative topics for research or composition. *Lochinvar Guides* are intended to stimulate readers to want to learn more, so we are happy if you are stimulated to research something of personal meaning to you.

Literature Circle Approaches in the *Lochinvar Guides*

Classroom teachers often use Literature Circles in order to provide their students with a full reading experience. In such a case, a class is divided into small groups, or "circles," and as the days roll by, students take turns serving as Illustrator, Connector, Word Master, Quiz Master, or Researcher. In the *Lochinvar Guides,* the technique has been adapted somewhat to make it useful in either a classroom or a home-school setting. It is our fondest hope that students will develop a lifelong desire to go beyond the text at hand and broaden out to other resources, including, in the case of Illustrator, their own imaginations. Below is a brief explanation of each approach.

Illustration—One of the differences between watching a movie and reading a book is that viewers passively absorb an image imposed by another person while readers actively create pictures in their own minds. This is one of the great pleasures of reading—seeing with "the mind's eye." In works of nonfiction, the imaging goes beyond entertainment, which is perhaps the focus of literature, and helps the reader better understand people, places, and events from real life—battlefields and battle formations, for example, or Greek architecture or Roman roads. To this end, students are asked from time to time to examine a particular passage for its visual detail and render it on a piece of paper (stick figures are altogether fine). Examples might be to sketch a person who has gotten himself into a predicament, a genealogical chart, a map, a graph, etc.

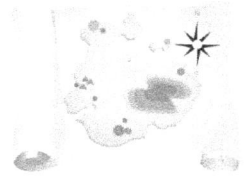

Research—Sometimes an author will introduce a topic but not provide all the details. In these cases, students directed to find out more about a topic in a library or on the Internet. For example, Benjamin Franklin lived in Pennsylvania, where there was a large Quaker population often mentioned by Franklin in his autobiography. A suitable research topic would be to discover some of the basic facts about the Quaker religion.

Connection—"Great minds think alike," runs an old saying. They may not always think exactly alike, but they do often think about the same things. For example, while reading a first-person account of a war experience, one might come across the explanation of a

deception that was played on the enemy. This might put the reader in mind of the Trojan horse narrative from the *Iliad* or the *Aeneid*. This link-up would connect the text with a work of literature, but connections can also be made with current events, historic events, aphorisms, music, movies—or even personal experience.

Bible Connection—One special kind of connection is, of course, connection with Scripture. In 2 Corinthians 10:5, Paul states, "We destroy arguments and every lofty opinion raised against the knowledge of God, and take every thought captive to obey Christ." Therefore, as part of their intellectual life, Christian readers frequently ask, "Does the message of this work comport with or contradict Scripture?" Even when reading works of the ancient philosophers who did not have the advantage of revealed religion, we sometimes come across statements that are markedly prescient regarding the biblical narrative. The narrative referred to as "Plato's Cave," for example, is astonishingly insightful. As Cyril of Jerusalem put it so long ago, the Father, the Son, and the Holy Spirit "lighteneth *every* man coming into the world"[1] (emphasis mine). Discovering glimpses of ultimate truth (or the lack thereof) among both ancient and modern writers makes familiarity with and application of Scripture an invaluable tool for the believer.

Mortimer Adler's 102 Great Ideas—Mortimer Adler's contribution to the study of the Great Books was monumental. A more detailed explanation of the use of his 102 Great Ideas appears in the pages that follow. Here it is only necessary to say that, like works of literature, great works of nonfiction also deal with universal themes—ideas that are relevant at all times to all people. From time to time, students are asked to examine a passage by a particular writer in light of one of the topics from Adler's list, such as War, Progress, Courage, Law, or Justice. In this way, they will be able to engage in what Adler called the Great Conversation of western civilization.

The 102 Great Ideas Identified by Mortimer Adler

1. Angel
2. Animal
3. Aristocracy
4. Art
5. Astronomy and Cosmology
6. Beauty
7. Being
8. Cause
9. Chance
10. Change
11. Citizen
12. Constitution
13. Courage
14. Custom and Convention
15. Definition
16. Democracy
17. Desire
18. Dialectic
19. Duty
20. Education
21. Element
22. Emotion
23. Eternity
24. Evolution
25. Experience
26. Family

27. Fate
28. Form
29. God
30. Good and Evil
31. Government
32. Habit
33. Happiness
34. History
35. Habit
36. Hypothesis
37. Idea
38. Immortality
39. Induction
40. Infinity
41. Judgment
42. Justice
43. Knowledge
44. Labor
45. Language
46. Law
47. Liberty
48. Life and Death
49. Logic
50. Love
51. Man (Humankind)
52. Mathematics

53. Matter
54. Mechanics
55. Medicine
56. Memory and Imagination
57. Metaphysics
58. Mind
59. Monarchy
60. Nature
61. Necessity and Contingency
62. Oligarchy
63. One and Many
64. Opinion
65. Opposition
66. Philosophy
67. Physics
68. Pleasure and Pain
69. Poetry
70. Principle
71. Progress
72. Prophecy
73. Prudence
74. Punishment
75. Quality
76. Quantity
77. Reasoning
78. Relation

79. Religion
80. Revolution
81. Rhetoric
82. Same and Other
83. Science
84. Sense
85. Sign and Symbol
86. Sin
87. Slavery
88. Soul
89. Space
90. State
91. Temperance
92. Theology
93. Time
94. Truth
95. Tyranny and Despotism
96. Universal and Particular
97. Virtue and Vice
98. War and Peace
99. Wealth
100. Will
101. Wisdom
102. World

The Use of Adler's 102 Great Ideas in *Lochinvar Guides to Classic Works of Nonfiction*

As part of his effort to improve education by improving the way students think, the American philosopher and educator Mortimer Adler (1902-2001), founded, with Max Weissman, the Center for the Study of the Great Ideas. In doing so, scholars identified what Adler called the 102 Great Ideas, which he defined as "the ideas basic and indispensable to understanding ourselves, our society, and the world in which we live."[2]

Mortimer Adler

In their English classes at school, students are usually introduced to the concept of *theme,* that is, the idea which a given work of literature develops. In this respect, Adler's list can be quite helpful. In *Romeo and Juliet* by William Shakespeare, for example, students might discuss exactly what it was that made things go so wrong for the young, "star-crossed" lovers. Were they really destined by their stars, or were they ruined by the bad choices of the humans in the story? These questions correspond to at least two of the Great Ideas on Adler's list: Fate and Cause. Therefore, the list of the 102 Great Ideas can certainly help a student respond to the theme underlying a great work of literature.

But what about great works of nonfiction, especially the primary sources of history—autobiographies, eyewitness accounts of history, philosophical treatises, laws and charters, *enchiridia*, and the like? Can Adler's list of the Great Ideas help the student with these works? We believe so. It is the purpose of the *Lochinvar Guides to Classic Works of Nonfiction* to help students to think about the ideas underlying the important nonfiction works of the western canon. Specifically, we hope students will learn, first, to read not only for facts, but for ideas; and, secondly, not only for comprehension of the ideas, but for a rigorous examination of them.

Why "rigorous examination"? *Lochinvar Guides* are written from a classical and Christian point of view. We wholeheartedly agree with the apostle Paul, who pointed out that we no longer have to be "tossed back and forth by the waves, and blown here and there by every wind of teaching" nor need we fall victim to "the cunning and craftiness of people in their deceitful scheming" (Eph. 4:14).

What is more, we are even commanded to evaluate ideas: "Do not despise prophecies, but test everything; hold fast what is good" (I Thess. 5:20-21). And the

God of Abraham, Isaac, and Jacob has shown that he does not shy away from any test. In the Old Testament, for example, we see that God allowed Jacob to wrestle with him; and in the New Testament, we see that the risen Jesus allowed the doubting disciple Thomas to examine his wounds. In neither case was the mere mortal—so full of questions—judged or condemned. Rather, God was not offended because he knew that he would triumph in any contest regarding Truth.

In short, we are not only encouraged, but even commanded to question the voices in the wind, and, because Judeo-Christian Scripture is solid ground, we know we can use it as our bedrock in the storm. That is why you will be asked in these study guides not only to search for a writer's ideas and to test them by using reason and logic, but also to evaluate them in the light of Scripture.

One last question remains: When we refer to the *Great Ideas*, what exactly is meant by the word *great*? For example, noticing that Slavery is on the list, one might say that slavery was not at all a great idea, that it was—and remains—a horrible idea. To sort this all out, we can turn to the work of Peter Mark Roget (1779-1869), the creator of *Roget's International Thesaurus*, who suggested the following synonyms for the word *great*: *important, consequential, prominent; noteworthy, memorable; weighty, solemn, serious;* and, for the word *weighty*, he suggests *influential*.[3] All of these synonyms help explain Adler's application of the word *great*. He did not necessarily mean each Idea was *wonderful*, but that it was *consequential, weighty,* or *influential*—for better or for worse. It is in this sense, then, that we can see that Evil, Slavery, and Tyranny properly belong among Adler's 102 Great Ideas alongside Truth, Beauty, and Love.

Recommended Text

There are many editions of Asser's *Life of Alfred* available, both online and in print. We have divided the readings into sections that can be used with any version of the text, but for easiest reference, we recommend the Penguin Classics edition (ISBN 978-0140444094).

Historical Background

The person we know as Alfred the Great, king of England, was known to his own people as Alfred, king of Wessex. Similarly, the island we know as England was called Britain by the Romans and was still so called when Asser wrote his biography of Alfred in 893, calling Alfred "ruler of all the Christians of the island of Britain, king of the Angles and Saxons." So, immediately we see the need for some clarification: Britain, Christian Britain, Wessex, Angles, Saxons, England—what exactly is what?

To understand the complexities of ethnic and national identity at the time of Alfred (849-899), it is necessary to go even farther back in time to the period when the Romans controlled Britain from AD 43-410. The ethnic identity of the original people of Britain was Celtic, so the terms *Briton* and *Celt* become interchangeable when discussing the Roman period. Though other Roman emperors had made attempts at taking Britain, it was not until AD 43 when the Emperor Claudius finally subdued the Britons that one could speak of the Roman control of Britain. Britain remained part of the Roman Empire until AD 410 when the Roman soldiers in Britain were called back to defend Rome against the barbarian invasions which ultimately brought it down.

During the 367-year period of Roman rule, the Britons had become quite Romanized, living in cities and accepting the civilizing influences of both the Roman Empire and Christianity, which entered Britain as early as the second century AD. Consequently, the Britons in the Roman areas of the island were no longer the aggressive tribes that the Romans had encountered early on. Perhaps we should not be surprised then that, once the Romans were gone, the less civilized Celtic (or British) tribes—especially the Picts from Scotland—poured into Romanized Britain in an attempt to take it over. The "citified" Romano-Britons were not able to withstand the attacks and sought help from the Germanic peoples, the same war-like people the Romans were fending off on the continent.

As a result, in 449, the British king Vortigern extended an invitation to two Germanic leaders, Hengist and Horsa, desiring their assistance in repelling the Celts. Because of this, three Germanic tribes called the Angles, the Saxons, and the Jutes arrived in Britain to do battle with the Celtic invaders. Though the Britons did have some victories against these Germanic tribes, by 577 the Celts had been pushed back largely into Wales, Cornwall (southwestern Britain), and Scotland, leaving most of what we now call England to the Angles, Saxons, and Jutes, who had, by this time, decided to stay. Ultimately, it was the name of the Angles who gave their name to the "new Britain"—*Angle-land*, or England—and the language spoken there—*Angle-isch*, or English.

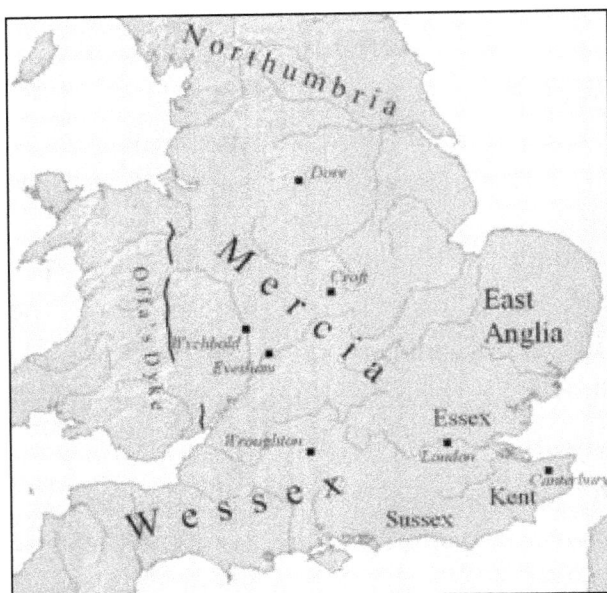

The Anglo-Saxon Heptarchy

The Jutes settled largely in southeastern Britain in the area still known as Kent (see map). The Saxons settled in areas whose names signify Saxon habitation—Wessex (West Saxons), Essex (East Saxons), and Sussex (South Saxons). The Angles settled largely in the remaining areas of the island.

By 600, there were seven distinct kingdoms of Germanic origin—East Anglia, Mercia [pronounced MER-sē-ə], Northumbria, Wessex, Essex, Kent, and Sussex. They are known as the Anglo-Saxon Heptarchy (from the Greek roots *hept-* (seven) and *-archy* (rule).

In the late eighth century, King Offa of Mercia built a wall, called Offa's Dyke, which separated the Anglo-Saxon people from the Celts residing in Wales (see map above).

When Asser took up his narrative, he began with the year 849, the year of Alfred's birth, at which time Alfred's father, Æthelwulf, was king of Wessex. As he progressed, he told about Alfred's various conflicts with other Anglo-Saxon kingdoms, the Celts in Wales, and a new invader—the Vikings.

The student is advised, while reading, to use various resources such as a genealogical tree of the kings of Wessex (PENGUIN 62), a map of the Anglo-Saxon Heptarchy (see above), and a map showing the movements of the Vikings in England (PENGUIN 59-61). Such tools can significantly improve comprehension of nonfiction works.

A Note on Ancient and Medieval Biography

In the nineteenth century, a German historian named Leopold von Ranke (1795-1886) established the guidelines which have been used by professional historians and biographers ever since. Ranke believed that history should be written from what are called primary sources—material written during the time under discussion, such as letters, diaries, images, and documents, which serve to verify that the biographer is being truthful.

Leopold von Ranke

Biographies from the ancient and medieval periods were not so evidentiary. In the Middle Ages, for example, many authors wrote lives of the saints. These works would often include omens, miracles (sometimes bordering on magic), and exaggerated depictions of holiness—a type of writing called *hagiography* (from the Greek *hagio-*, or holy, and *-graphy*, or writing). This methodology transferred to the writing of royal biographies, which were typically written by an admirer, even an appointed admirer, and had as its purpose the praise of a powerful and important person. Though all leaders are subject to the law of sin, the weaknesses, cruelties, and excesses of the subjects of a medieval biography would be entirely overlooked. Only the good was recorded, and sometimes even that was exaggerated. In short, we could say that the medieval royal biography was more akin to hagiography than to a modern critical biography, which would explore both strengths and weaknesses.

This is not to say that such works cannot be trusted. They serve as significant sources of information for those of us who are removed so far in time and distance from the subject of the biography. However, it is important to keep in mind that their purpose was to praise, not to evaluate, and we can profit from the practice of "reading between the lines" to perceive spots where, say, the king's enemies might have had a different interpretation of the king's actions than that held by the king's appointed court historian. Such a practice can enhance the pleasure of reading nonfiction primary source material and send the reader off on new adventures to seek "the whole truth."

Part 1: Family and Youth

Scope

This reading covers Sections 1-50.

Terms

In this and subsequent chapters, the terms, words, and identifications are presented in alphabetical order.

1. abbess (ĂB-əs) (n.) – the woman in charge of a convent (or abbey) of nuns

2. ealdorman (ĂL-dər-mən or ÄL-dər-mən) (n.) – the chief officer of a shire in the Anglo-Saxon period (from the fifth century to 1066)

3. heir apparent (n. phr.) – in a society where rulers inherit their right to govern, the person next in the line of succession (e.g., a prince or princess)

4. minster (MĬN-stər) (n.) – the name given a church that grew out of a community of monks living in a monastery; later, a cathedral

5. services of the hours (n. phr.) – the official set of prayers uttered eight times a day on the hour, consisting of psalms, hymns, and readings of prayers

6. shield-wall (n.) – a military formation in which the soldiers stand shoulder to shoulder, overlapping each other's shields in order to create a wall of defense

7. thegn (thān) (n.) – in Anglo-Saxon England, a feudal lord's officer or retainer, who normally held lands of the lord and provided military service; sometimes spelled *thane*

8. triune (trī-OON) (adj.) – three in one; a reference to the Trinity in the Christian religion

Words

1. deploy (dĭ-PLŌY) (v.) – to arrange soldiers in a battle line

2. desist (dĭ-SĬST) (v.) – to abstain; to refrain from

3. incur (ĭn-KUR) (v.) – to bring on oneself, as of scorn or disapproval

4. iniquitous (ĭn-ĬK-wə-təs) (adj.) – evil, wrong, base

5. verbosity (vər-BŎS-ə-tē) (n.) – wordiness

Identifications

1. Gaul – Celtic tribal area now occupied by France and its neighbors

2. Goths – an East Germanic tribe

3. Jutes – a Germanic tribe from the Jutland Peninsula and part of the North Frisian coast

4. Offa's Dyke – an earthwork that ran 150 miles between the Anglo-Saxon kingdom of Mercia and the Welsh kingdom of Powys, named for Offa, a seventh-century Mercian king

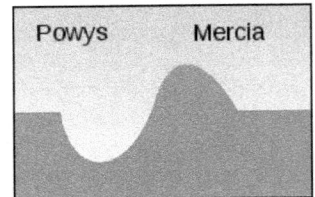

5. Picts – a Celtic people from the north and east of Scotland

6. Pope Leo – Leo IV, Roman Catholic pope from 847 to 855, famous for organizing Italy's defense against Arab pirates

Diction: Parenthetical Remarks

One feature of Asser's writing style is the use of the parenthetical remark, an explanation or a comment placed inside parentheses for further edification of the reader. In fact, the very first sentence in the narrative employs this technique:

Use of parentheses:

> "In the year of the Lord's Incarnation 849 Alfred, king of the Anglo-Saxons, was born at the royal estate called Wantage, in the district known as Berkshire (*which is so called from Berroc Wood, where the box-tree grows very abundantly*)" (PENGUIN SEC. 1).

The detail about the origin of the name *Berkshire* is not directly related to the narrative, but Asser apparently felt that the detail was instructive. Therefore, he placed it inside parentheses, which reveals a detail while still de-emphasizing it.

The same effect is sometimes accomplished with different punctuation marks, thus:

Use of dashes:

"However, while King Æthelwulf was lingering overseas, even for so short a time, a disgraceful episode—*contrary to the practice of all Christian men*—occurred in the western part of Selwood" (PENGUIN SEC. 12).

Use of commas:

"Spurred on by these words, *or rather by divine inspiration*, and attracted by the beauty of the initial letter in the book, Alfred spoke. . ." (PENGUIN SEC. 23).

As indicated at the beginning of the study guide in "A Note on Ancient and Medieval Biography," writers in earlier epochs would often insert remarks which would nudge the reader in the direction of a favorable opinion of the hero of the narrative or an unfavorable opinion of the villain. In the second and third examples above, we see that Asser often employed the parenthetical remark in this way.

The exercise that follows places focus on the different purposes for which Asser uses parenthetical remarks.

Exercise: Decoding Parenthetical Remarks

Directions: Read each of the excerpts below and, in the space provided, indicate what you consider to be the purpose of the parenthetical remark. Is it, for example, to express an opinion, to provide a definition—or something else?

1. "The Vikings spent the winter on the Isle of Sheppey (*which means 'island of sheep'*)" (SEC. 3).

2. "After these things had happened there, the Viking army moved on to Surrey (*a district situated on the southern bank of the River Thames, to the west of Kent*) (PENGUIN SEC. 5).

3. "When, therefore, King Æthelwulf returned from Rome, the entire nation was so delighted (*as was fitting*) at the arrival of their lord that, had he allowed it, they would have been willing to eject his grasping son Æthelbald. . ." (SEC. 13).

4. Eadburh "was ejected from the nunnery on Charlemagne's orders and shamefully spent her life in poverty and misery until her death; so much so that in the end, accompanied by a single slave boy (*as I have heard from many who saw her*) and begging every day, she died a miserable death in Pavia" (SEC. 15).

5. Alfred "was greatly loved, more than all his brothers, by his father and mother—*indeed, by everybody*—with a universal and profound love . . ." (SEC. 22).

Questions

1. What seafaring power was constantly raiding and invading the Anglo-Saxon regions at this time? (SEC. 3)

2. What religion was practiced by Alfred's parents? (SEC. 5, 8)

3. Alfred was not the eldest son in the family. How did it come to pass that he became the king? (SEC. 18, 74, 41)

4. While King Æthelwulf (Alfred's father) was in Rome, what did Æthelbald (Alfred's brother) do? (SEC. 12)

5. Whom did Æthelbald marry after his father, King Æthelwulf, died? (SEC. 17)

6. Alfred's mother once told her sons that they could compete for a prize. What was it? What did Alfred do to win it? (SEC. 23)

7. What was Alfred's first challenge after becoming king? (SEC. 42)

8. On the next page, answer the series of graduated questions, carrying the facts forward to the inductive reasoning question at the end.

Fact 1: What did Pope Leo do when Æthelwulf took his youngest son, Alfred, to Rome? (SEC. 8)

Fact 2: Which son won his mother's challenge and received the book of poetry? (SEC. 23)

Fact 3: Was Alfred sincerely religious? Explain your answer. (SEC. 24-25)

Fact 4: What desire was young Alfred not able to fulfill—and why? (SEC. 24-25)

Fact 5: In the battle at Ashdown, which brother arrived first, and in what condition were his troops? What desire was young Alfred not able to fulfill? Why not? (SEC. 37)

Fact 6: What did Alfred do when his brother, the king, would not leave off prayer in a tent? (SEC. 38)

Inductive Reasoning: What do you think Asser was trying to say about Alfred by providing these six narratives?

The Great Ideas: Custom and Convention

One of the 102 Great Ideas laid out by Mortimer Adler is **Custom and Convention**. In Section 13, we see that an issue arose in the kingdom when King Æthelwulf wanted his queen, Judith, the daughter of Charles the Bald (a descendant of Charlemagne) to "sit beside him on the royal throne until the end of his life, though this was contrary to the (wrongful) custom of that people." This is a bit confusing, so let's slow down and try to dig out what Asser is saying here.

1. In Æthelwulf's time, was the custom to have the queen sit on the throne with her husband or not? What was the queen called? (SEC. 13)

2. According to Asser, was that practice the correct or the wrong custom, according to the customs of the Germanic peoples? What did the Germanic people usually do in this regard? (SEC. 13)

3. Briefly explain generally what had happened that caused the Anglo-Saxons to do away with the traditional practice of the Germanic people? (SEC. 13)

An Anglo-Saxon Queen

The Great Ideas: Religion

One of the 102 Great Ideas laid out by Mortimer Adler is **Religion**. In the Anglo-Saxon period, Church and State worked together hand in glove. Please examine Section 16 to discover how Æthelwulf used part of the royal treasury for religious and charitable uses.

1. A *hide* was a measure of land. For every 10 hides in Alfred's kingdom, what was to be done? (SEC. 16)

2. Some money was to be sent to Rome, the seat of the pope. How much and why? (SEC. 16)

3. With your classmate(s), discuss whether either, neither, or both of these measures are Biblical uses of the believers' treasury, and jot down what you conclude in the space provided. Include a Scripture reference to support your ideas.

An Anglo-Saxon mancus (gold coin)

Part 2: Fighting the Vikings

Scope

Please notice that the Penguin edition of Asser's *Life of Asser* indicates in a footnote at Section 51 that scholars are unsure whether that passage was actually written by Asser. Therefore, this reading assignment will cover Sections 52-74.

Terms

1. chrisom [KRĬZ-əm] (n.) – the cloth which covered the face or head during baptism so that the chrism (anointing oil) would not rub off; the baptismal gown

2. nones [nōnz] (n.) – according to the daily cycle of prayers of the Roman Catholic Church, the ninth hour (3:00 p.m.)

3. vespers [VĚS-pərz] (n.) – according to the daily cycle of prayers of the Roman Catholic Church, sunset

4. tribute [TRĬB-yūt] (n.) – payment made periodically by one king to a more powerful king, as a sign of dependence

Words

5. accede [ăk-SĒD] (v.) – give in; agree to a demand

6. carnal [KÄR-nəl] (adj.) – of the flesh, especially of bodily pleasure

7. cursorily [KUR-sər-ə-lē] (adv.) – in a hasty, superficial manner

8. malady [MĂL-ə-dē] (n.) – ailment

9. piles [pīlz] (n.) – common term for the medical condition hemorrhoids (called *ficus* [FĒ-kəs] in some translations)

10. prostrate [PRŎS-trāt] (adj.) – lying face down on the floor or ground in a manner of humility

11. venerable [VĔN-ər-ə-bəl] (adj.) – respected for age and wisdom

12. wont [wənt] (adj.) – accustomed to (referring to habitual activities)

Identifications

1. Alemanni [äl-ə-MÄ-nē or äl-ə-MÄ-nī] – a group of Germanic tribes who inhabited the area between the Rhine, Main, and Danube rivers

2. Egbert's Stone – a modern English rendering of the Anglo-Saxon word *Ecgbryhtesstan*, a site now believed to have been located in the shire of Somerset; named for King Egbert of Wessex, who ruled from 802-839

3. Francia [FRĂNK-ē-ə] – the area inhabited by the Franks, a Germanic tribe; located in what is now France and neighboring regions; in the ninth century, *Gaul* and *Francia* would have been interchangeable terms, though the areas were not exactly coterminous

4. Franks [frănks] – a Germanic tribe that settled in the area the Romans called Gaul and for whom the country of France is named

5. Frisians [FRĒ-zhənz] – the Germanic tribe that inhabited the coastal region of the North Sea in what today is the Netherlands

6. Ghent [gĕnt] [hard *g*] – a city in northwest Belgium, the region known as Flanders in Alfred's time

7. Thames [tĕmz] – the River Thames, a major river that flows through southern England [see map]

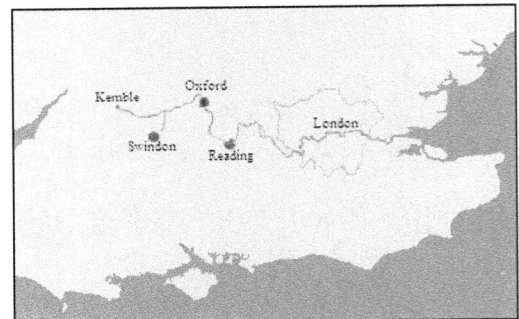

The Course of the Thames River

Questions

1. What does Asser reveal about Alfred's health? (SEC. 74)

2. Answer the series of graduated questions, carrying the facts forward to the inductive reasoning at the end.

Fact 1: What was the situation of Alfred and his men at the beginning of this reading? (SEC. 53)

Fact 2: Describe how things changed after the Battle of Edington. (SEC. 56)

Fact 3: How was Alfred's army able to improve its situation in 885? (SEC. 66)

Fact 4: How was Alfred able to build up his navy in 885? (SEC. 67)

Inductive Reasoning: What do these incidents show you about Alfred's military ability?

Mortimer Adler's Great Ideas: Pleasure and Pain

One of the 102 Great Ideas laid out by Mortimer Adler is **Pleasure and Pain.** In this reading, we learn about a life-long health problem that Alfred had (SEC. 74). Explain the problem, its onset, and its duration. Then summarize and comment on the spiritual dimension regarding the cause of and the response to the pain, as it is explained by Asser.

Research

To learn more about topics mentioned in this reading, research one of the topics below and write an essay no longer than one page, explaining in your own words, what you learned. On a second page, include illustrations (either photocopied from a book or cut-and-pasted from a web site on the Internet). In addition, identify the sources of your information and images, using the documentation style of the Modern Language Association (MLA), which is explained and exemplified below.

Topics:

- Viking ships

- King Alfred's navy

- Hunting in the Early Middle Ages

- Anglo-Saxon weddings

MLA Documentation:

- **Web Site:**

  o Author (last name first, if given)

  o Title of article (inside quotation marks)

  o Name of web site (in italics)

  o Date placed online (or, if not given, *n.d.* for *no date*)

  o Medium (Web)

     o Date accessed (European style)

Examples:

Levick, Ben. "Anglo-Saxon Military Organization." *Regia Anglorum.* 28 Mar. 2005. Web. 27 Jan. 2016.

Ross, David. "Ethelred, the Danes, and the Confessor." *Britain Express.* n.d. Web. 4 Feb. 2016.

- **Book:**

     o Author (last name first)

     o Title (in italics)

     o City of publication

     o Publisher

     o Year of publication

     o Medium (Print)

Example:

Walker, Ian W. *Harold: The Last Anglo-Saxon King.* Stroud: History, 1997. Print.

For a more detailed explanation of MLA style, you may wish to consult the *Purdue Online Writing Lab* (OWL) on the Internet.

Part 3: Building a Kingdom

Scope

This reading covers Sections 75-106.

Terms

1. fealty [FĒ-əl-tē] (n.) – the faithfulness of a vassal to his lord or of a subject to his king, a key element of medieval feudalism

2. reeve [rēv] (n.) – the administrative officer of a town or shire; the term "shire reeve" changed over time to create our word *sheriff.*

3. tonsured [TŎN-shərd] (adj.) – shaved on the crown of the head in preparation to become a monk

Words

1. abate [ə-BĀT] (v.) – to diminish, become less severe

2. admonition [ăd-mə-NĬ-shən] (n.) – advice to proceed cautiously, warning

3. albeit [äl-BĒ-ĭt] (adv.) – although, even if

4. cajole [kə-JŌL] (v.) – to persuade someone by using flattery or promises; to wheedle

5. causeway [KÄZ-wā] (n.) – a raised road over wet land or low water

6. luminary [LŪ-mə-nār-ē] (n.) – a person who is advanced in his field of study and has the respect of his or her peers

7. propitious [prō-PĬSH-əs] (adj.) – under favorable conditions

8. punt [pənt] (n.) – a shallow boat with a flat bottom propelled through the water by means of a pole

9. rudiments [RŪ-də-mənts] (n. pl.) – basic principles of a subject under study

10. taciturnity [tăs-ə-TƏR-nə-tē] (n.) – the state of being quiet or reserved in conversation

Identifications

1. Dyfed [DƏ-vəd] - a post-Roman Welsh kingdom in the farthest southwest corner of Wales

2. Mawr [mär] – a Welsh word meaning "Great"; thus, *Rhodri Mawr* means *Rhodri the Great*

3. Pope Gregory – Gregory I, the medieval pope who served from 590 to 604; also known as Gregory the Great

Questions

1. How did Asser assist Alfred in his desire to keep meaningful passages from books? (SEC. 88; PENGUIN END NOTE 211)

2. Answer the series of graduated questions on the next page, carrying the facts forward to the inductive reasoning at the end.

Fact 1: What various people groups submitted willingly to Alfred's rule? (SEC. 76)

Fact 2: What four well-educated men came to assist King Alfred, and from which Anglo-Saxon kingdom did they come? (SEC. 77)

Fact 3: Who else came to enhance the cultural level of Alfred's kingdom, and where were they from? (SEC. 78)

Fact 4: From what country did Asser himself come? (SEC. 79)

Fact 5: What Welsh kingdoms submitted to Alfred? What did Anarawd ap Rhodri do? (SEC. 80)

Fact 6: To whom did Alfred entrust the governance of London? (SEC. 83)

Fact 7: With what distant places did Alfred establish communications? (SEC. 91)

Fact 8: What three other people groups are mentioned regarding Alfred's cultural efforts? (SEC. 94)

Inductive Reasoning: What is Asser telling his readers about Alfred by including this long list of people and groups?

The Great Ideas: Education

One of the 102 Great Ideas laid out by Mortimer Adler is **Education.** From the inductive reasoning exercise above, we see King Alfred's desire to elevate the level of scholarship and culture of the people he governed. In this regard, Asser gives us information about education reforms among the Anglo-Saxons of Alfred's time. Please answer the questions below in order to understand the depth of Alfred's challenge and what he did to improve matters.

1   Did Alfred educate all of his children, including his daughters? (SEC. 75)

2. Were children of "lesser birth" educated along with the children of the nobility? (SEC. 75)

3. What was taught in Alfred's schools? (SEC. 75)

4. In addition to teaching academic subjects, how did Alfred's schools foster good character? (SEC. 75)

5. Besides his own children, whose sons were educated in the royal household? (SEC. 76)

6. At times, did Alfred himself teach the students? (SEC. 76)

7. After learning to read English, what other language did Alfred himself learn to read and write? (SEC. 87)

8. How did Alfred finance his schools? (SEC. 102)

9. What did Alfred require of his judges, with respect to learning? (SEC. 106)

10. Were slaves taught to read in Alfred's kingdom? (SEC. 106)

11. In Asser's last passage, what does Asser reveal about how the judges and elders encouraged the younger generation with regard to education? (SEC. 106)

The Great Ideas: Good and Evil

One of the 102 Great Ideas laid out by Mortimer Adler is **Good and Evil.** We like to think that people of faith behave in a manner pleasing to the Lord. But Asser provides a narrative about a priest and deacon from Gaul who did not do so. After reading the narrative (SEC. 96-97), answer this question: In Asser's opinion, what was the cause of their evil, and how was it avenged?

The Great Ideas: Self and Other

One of the 102 Great Ideas laid out by Mortimer Adler is **Self and Other.** While narrating the events surrounding the attempted murder of an abbot, Asser stated that "the two betrayers of their lord (*in the manner of the Jews*) all ran helter-skelter to the doors of the church" [emphasis added] (SEC. 97). This is an apparent comparison to Judas, who betrayed Jesus on the night of his arrest and trial. Throughout the Middle Ages, the relationship between Christians and Jews was a troubled one, which produced rhetoric and violence that is hard for us to understand today. European Jews were perceived by the dominant community as "other," not like "us," an attitude which sometimes lead to serious misunderstanding and persecution.

To explore this issue, do one or both of the exercises below, as your teacher desires.

1. Dr. Thomas F. Madden of the University of St. Louis has written an article entitled "The Church and the Jews in the Middle Ages," which is available on the Internet. Read the article and then summarize how the worldview of the Middle Ages affected the way different people groups looked at each other.

   URL: <https://www.catholicculture.org/culture/library/view.cfm?recnum=4705>

2. In the United States, to deter and punish violence motivated by hatred of a group perceived as "other," legislation has been passed making such acts a "hate crime." Canada has gone even farther, creating "hate speech" laws which restrict the freedom of speech otherwise guaranteed in their Constitution. To explore this issue, discuss with your class the various issues involved here:

   a. Is a certain wariness between peoples of different groups natural, or is it learned?

   b. Is a "hate crime" determinable, since one cannot really know what is in another person's heart?

   c. Where free speech is concerned, how can one distinguish between the normal discourse between contrasting worldviews, on the one hand, and hate propaganda on the other?

   d. Was a logical fallacy involved in Asser's comment in Section 97 of his text? Explain.

Composition

Very few monarchs go down in history with "the Great" attached to their names. Write a composition in which you explain three or four key reasons why Alfred is known as "the Great." Begin by making an outline, and support each point with examples from Asser's text.

Notes

[1] "The Fifth Theological Oration on the Holy Spirit." Christian Classics Ethereal Library. 13 July 2005. Web. 22 Jan. 2016.
[2] "Philosophy Is Everybody's Business." *TheGreatIdeas.org*. The Great Ideas. Center for the Study of the Great Ideas: A Synoptical Approach to the Great Books and Practical Philosophy. Web. 12 Jan. 2016.
[3] Roget. 3rd ed. New York: Crowell, 1962. 437, 84.

www.ingramcontent.com/pod-product-compliance
Lightning Source LLC
Chambersburg PA
CBHW081154040426

42445CB00015B/1883